TOSKA

TOSKA

Love. Life. Loss

MANSI HITESH

PARTRIDGE
A Penguin Random House Company

Sketch: Arani Halder
Pictures for Life and Everything else: Sumit Sharma
Picture for Loss: Arvinder Singh Rooprai

ISBN: Hardcover   978-1-4828-1211-4
             Softcover   978-1-4828-1212-1
             Ebook   978-1-4828-1210-7

To order additional copies of this book, contact
Partridge India
000 800 10062 62
www.partridgepublishing.com/india
orders.india@partridgepublishing.com

Also by Mansi Hitesh
Bizarre

Foreword

Mansi and my daughters were 'colony friends' which as everybody knows, is as good as being cousins.

Though she is quite the young lady now, I remember her as a naughty, bright-eyed little monkey, so adept at climbing up trees and walls and door frames that my husband used to call her spidermansi.

Her poetry contains that same exploring, gravity-defying quality.

I am sure you will thoroughly enjoy leafing through these pages :-)

ANUJA CHAUHAN
Author of "The Zoya Factor"
and "Those Pricey Thakur Girls"

For BlackSnow

Acknowledgements

Gratitude, leaves us humbled. As I sit down to pen the names of those who I want to thank, a smile plays on my face. I feel so content, to have the typical Indian family, with it's daily dose of drama, food loving 'bhukkad' friends, with their 'tana-bana'. A few special friends, who must not be named. Some delectable eye candy with their raised eyebrows, spectacled teachers, with their words of wisdom, and who can forget, the occasional greeters. The world I live in, is full of such unique characters, that I realize, there's no need to name these beautiful, legendary people. They all recognize themselves from the hopefully, accurate descriptions.

Love you guys!
-Mansi

Toska

"No single word in English renders all the shades of toska. At its deepest and most painful, it is a sensation of great spiritual anguish, often without any specific cause. At less morbid levels it is a dull ache of the soul, a longing with nothing to long for, a sick pining, a vague restlessness, mental throes, yearning. In particular cases it may be the desire for somebody of something specific, nostalgia, love-sickness. At the lowest level it grades into ennui, boredom."

-Vladmir Nabokov

LOVE

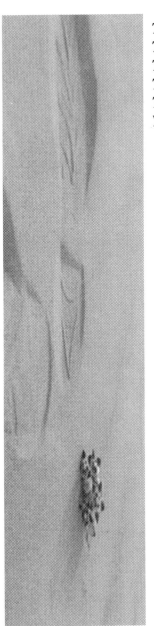

A PATCH UP

Head to heart,
Just one me,
It's just a start,
Of what could be,
A fusion, a mix,
A little fix,
No more sorrows,
Just hopes for tomorrow,
No more tears,
Just bidding goodbye to fears,
Feels peaceful
And calm,
As if I'm cradled
In God's loving arm,
This inner silence,
After violence,
Is it true?
Could I have become more me,
And less you?
This happiness is delighting,
The silence, frightening,
Is this the silence before a storm?

A VAIN VOW

Silence,
It's a vow,
A promise of truth,
The vain curse
of staying mute,
Of veiling the thoughts,
That ache to meet the tongue,
To hide and burn,
The feelings that were so young,
To curb the constant ramble
Of words aching to flow,
To ignore the heart's attempts
And let the darkness grow,
To let those melodies remain unrequited,
To hush my happiness,
With a mere "that's it"
This is the wave that washes over me,
As the secret in me dies,
This is what this vow means to me,
Though it doesn't reach my eyes.

ALLURE

Silence fills up the emptiness,
The hollows of my remains,
An alien emotion,
Breaks me,
And overpowers every strain,
Anger seduces words,
But fails to go all the way,
For silence will never allow,
For words to say,
The future seems to burn,
And ignites the way,
Fixed to my roots, my place
Is where I want to stay,
There are things to be done,
But they just end in one,
Sorrowful escape of the truth,
The secrets of which,
May crumble my youth.

AU REVOIR

A lingering weariness,
That's finally crashed over me,
I've severed our love,
I've withered the glee,
Lost is the shine,
Gone is the longing,
Of saying 'ever thine',
Estranged is the love,
Which we once termed as life,
Gone is the time,
It left and cut us,
'Twas the knife,
There's a rift that's arisen
To depart, I'm driven
And although it's a sin,
I hope I'm forgiven.

BLISS

Echoes that glide,
To cover hope's rays
Voices that blur,
And blacken my gaze,
Shrills that shiver,
And open my heart made of timber,
Whispers that linger,
Filling arrows in hatred's quiver,
A silence,
That's filled with notes,
A symphony of the pain,
The loathe,
A passion that ceases to exist,
That paves the path,
To eternal bliss.

BOUND

See the light,
In his eyes,
As if the color will suffice,
Feel his smile,
Warm me enough to tread a thousand miles,
A lock of his hair,
The sound of his voice,
They leave me no choice,
In his spell,
I'm going under,
All I can do is wonder,
Of what could be
The happiness, the glee,
The future, that doesn't want to greet me,
A vision so distant,
Yet so close,
Will it ever be reailty,
who knows,
All I know,
Is someday, my feelings I'll show,
And I'll be set free,
Of the chains and bounds,
Of a future,
That will never be.

BURNING CANDLE

Creeping in a corner,
Of this darkened room
Resides a ray of light,
That helps get me through
It helps me survive,
Although it flickers
Its heat lingers on,
It's light may be small
But its impact is strong,
It burns my fear,
Bit by bit,
It rages on,
No amount of heat
Can wither it,
Is it an illusion?
Keeping me alive,
Is it my soul?
Fighting to strive,
Is it just hope?
Burning away the binding ropes,
Or is it these words,
Making my fear fly away like birds
Whatever it is,
It's making me defiant
Even if it's wax
Is my heart.

CHANCE

I lay here under blackness,
Wide awake
Thinking about the choices,
The chances I have to take
The path that lays ahead,
Is not an easy tread
There are twists and turns
A risk of getting burns,
A danger of being bitten,
An offer of being smitten
A present, that can never be repaid,
A will, that cannot be swayed
A promise, that's become mine to honor,
Binds have caught me in a corner
A future that's mine to take,
A decision,
I cannot make.

DEVIL KISSED

Death seemed,
Like a distant mystery,
'Till I was haunted by your face,
And I wished to
Become a part of its ancient history
It felt so surreal
To feel your breath
Make me tremble,
Every broken and shattered dream
You re-assembled,
You clouded my vision,
I saw the world
Only to find you
somewhere
In it's wilted confusion
Your presence was intoxicating
My thirst for you; soul rending
Till one day, I touched you
And you turned to mist,
I realized my love for you
Was not bliss,
It was devil kissed.

DOWN LOW

L aughs and giggles,
We've had our share,
When I was in a mess,
You always helped,
You were always there,
We've captured pictures,
And memories too,
But who would have known,
That things would change so soon?
Those laughs seem distant,
They echo in my heart,
I try to connect the dots,
Where do I start?
I try to catch your eye,
But you're too sly,
You just ignore,
with a hint of hesitation,
'Heart—broken'
That's what's become my reputation,
Inside me, there's just frustration,
But what's the point,
Just like our good times,
This too will end up,
One day as a low point.

FORCE

There is a light,
    A source of power,
Which fixes my sorrow,
Every day, every hour,
A power with might,
But also, a feather touch,
It's presence around me,
I like very much,
I feel it healing me,
With a whisper through my hair,
It feels like I'm painless,
Like the hole in my heart,
Was never there,
it grasps my cold palms,
And guides me into,
Recovery's open arms,
It brightens,
It lightens the burden of my heart,
Hope and dreams,
It shelters, in my heart,
It makes every wrong right,
It makes me feel alive,
It fixes me,
Only if the energy was strong enough,
To make me forget thee.

HEAVEN

M on Cherie, c'est tout,
I'm done living in shadows of you
I'm done walking,
On your paved path
I'm done fighting your wars
And the aftermath,
I'm done sitting in silence
Simply witnessing the violence
Of your games,
Tell me, do you even remember my name?
You had me in a trance
You lost it
Your one and only chance
You lost my trust,
Fine, you can say you held my heart
Once, if you must
But no more will the
Show go on,
The weakened me
Has gone strong
So au revoir, mon cherie,
To fly away to heaven,
I'm ready.

I LOVE YOU

Everything feels so lively,
So new,
As fresh as drops of dew
Moments like these are few
I would experience one like it,
Who knew?
Everything's so silly
I feel so giddy
Feel like smiling,
The opposite of whining
I feel like flying
High in the sky,
I feel I can do it
Without giving it a try,
Every flower seems to bloom
Happiness takes the place of gloom
My heart goes boom!
I'm dancing to no music,
In my room
Why this laughter,
Why these expectations for
A 'happily ever after'
I don't know
And I don't want to
But whatever this magic is
Don't go,
Cuz I love you
That's all I need you to know.

I WONDER WHY

First our eyes would meet
 In sweet silence
Now between us
There's just violence
I wonder why?
I could think of a million reasons,
I could move on with the seasons,
But I can't
Cuz what I felt for you,
It was true
I wonder why love didn't suffice,
It's not like I didn't sacrifice
Or pour my heart out to you,
I wonder why I feel so empty
I wonder why I feel so robbed of me
Is it fair?
Would I dare?
I wonder why, I wonder why,
A tear doesn't fall from my eye
And even when it's over
I still try
I wonder why.

INVISIBLE

L imitless boundaries,
 Surround and envelop us,
An endless silence,
Grips and holds us,
A wordless plea,
Forms and escapes in the dust,
We're drowning in the shadows,
Of desire and lust,
Flightless, time is rendered,
As we revel in the past,
All our fears are surrendered,
As it breaks away, our ship's mast,
We've sailed and found,
There is no end,
We've tried and failed,
To survive the bend,
We've learnt and lost,
All there was to know,
We'll just spend eternity like this,
And hope it doesn't show.

LAWS OF ATTRACTION

You're sitting in a corner
   Whiling away your time
While I constantly day dream
About making you mine
You sit there effortlessly
Making my world spin around
I love you selflessly
But when I try to tell you
My words makes no sound
You turn the pages of a book
I quickly glance and steal a look
Is it true?
Am I becoming obsessed with you?
Or is it just attraction
Of love it's the slightest fraction,
What is this reaction?
You drum your fingers
Waiting for the bell to ring
I wonder if you can hear my heart sing
To the rhythm
If only someday we could meet
If only for a friendly greet
if only I could be your friend
But I realize, I'm wishing this would end,
To finish this, at the start,
And forget a boy like you
Ever stole my heart.

LIGHTENING

A faint voice,
Echoes in the dark,
I'm lost in memories of you,
I'm searching for the right remarks,
I'm searching,
For the words to say,
The ones you stole,
When you took my breath away,
I'm descending,
Into times I've lost,
Pretending like
It's free of cost,
Breathing in,
Your lingering presence,
Sinking in,
The evanescence,
Falling like the drops,
That are no stranger to the eye,
Calling,
As if you're my deity,
Feeling as empty as the sky.

LITHE

If love is so simple,
Why is it so prized?
If love is so precious,
Why do I feel victimized?
If love is a blessing,
Why does it haunt like a curse?
If love's a healer,
Why am I left with wounds to nurse?
If love is life,
Why are my breaths strained?
If love is flying,
Why are my feet constantly pained?
If love is real,
Why can't it be seen?
Is it a truth or lie,
Or something in between?

LOVE?

My smile's stretching,
Ear to ear
It's such bliss
To have you here,
There are a thousand words
I'd like to say,
But just to have this moment
The role of a friend I'll play,
But in my mind
I'm wishing the conversation would never end,
I'm biting my lip
Making a scar
that will take long to mend
I'm asking you,
If what I feel is right
I'm asking you,
If you'll stay the night
I'm imagining you in a tux all dressed up,
Twirling me around
In your arms I'm bundled up,
Tell me if I'm right
If you need help to fall asleep tonight,
Tell me, what can I do
Tell me how to fall in love
The way you want me to.

MARKED

M arked by silence,
Scarred by war,
Traced by the remains of the violence
Is our love,
Which can't go unignored
It's stray and lifeless,
What once was the thread of my life,
It lays among the ashes,
The spirit that once gave me triumph
It's dead and gone,
The melody that was my favorite song
It's buried in the past
Nothing's ever built to last
Then why do I try?
Why do I spend the last of my energy,
To cross you by
Why do I scream?
And wait for your voice
To echo back in this cave
Why do I dig my own grave?

MINE

P assing notes in secrecy
    You've changed my vision
It was clear to me,
'Till I wilted in confusion
Everything was in its place
I was leading the race
'Till you made me fall
Made me lose it all,
Lights were bright,
There were no foggy nights,
Till you broke my might,
And crushed the pieces on the floor
The splinters left my feet sore,
I can't feel myself anymore
Everything's numb
I'm breaking under the weight,
Of your thumb
But it's fine
As long as I'm yours
And you're mine.

PASSERBY

A few stolen moments,
Is all that we share,
They may be mere seconds,
But I don't care,
'Cuz these moments,
Make me feel alive,
Like I'd been living my life wrong,
But with you, everything is right,
It's amazing,
To feel so free,
Yet to feel I'm living in thee,
To feel so warm,
So calm,
To feel the only thing I need,
Is to be held in your arms,
To feel your presence,
Feel your touch,
Oh, mysterious friend
I like you very much.

POISON

D awn turns to dusk
As I leave three words unsaid,
Love, it's as heavy as musk,
Tears rain on my bed,
The poison, it's divine,
It's as much yours,
As it's mine,
It runs as deep,
As the secrets of our race,
It's as dark as a child's weep,
As fast, as the heart's pace,
It inflicts and kills,
All that I'd ever known,
For years on end,
I've hoped and hoped,
For you to know,
For it,
To not have shown.

REMINISCE

I 'll never kiss,
A pair of lips
Without wishing they were yours,
I'll never think of love
Without thinking of our course,
I'll never walk a lonely path
Without wanting you by my side,
I'll never sing those silly tunes
Without dedicating a note here or there,
Once or twice,
I'll never say, "yes" to a man
Without wondering if I'm saying no to you,
I'll never think of the future
Without considering how
Things could've been with you,
I'll think and remember
Till I forget,
Forgetting you, I'll never regret.

RIDE

M oving on,
Staying strong,
It's what I aim to do,
To start loving me,
More than I loved you,
To let go of every memory,
Anything that will grasp,
At that little corner of my heart,
And get me right back to the start,
To relive every memory,
And then erase,
Of you in my heart,
There shall be no trace,
No more hopes,
No more dreams,
No more shattering my soul,
No more silent screams,
No more of your humor,
No more of those precious moments,
I just have to get over,
Every syllable of admiration,
Every drop of regret,
I need to forget,
I need to survive,
But after facing your wrath,
I guess its recovery
That will be the easier ride.

SET FREE!

Time has gone by,
  After crying a flood
My eyes have run dry,
After a long time of sorrow
Suddenly, there's a bright new hope,
I'm not tightened by
The strength of your rope,
It's as if my scars
Are turning to skin,
It's like your perfume's gone from the air
And I'm finally breathing in
I feel like I'm letting go
Even though it's quite slow,
So farewell my dear
'Cuz you can't catch me here.

SPARKS FLY

The connection,
  The spark,
Those foolish concoctions
Brewed by our hearts
Those shy glances
That our eyes steal,
Those soft breaths,
with their warmth,
wounds they heal
Those melodies
With there notes ever so soft,
They give life to dreams,
Trains of thoughts,
Those tingles that
Wash over like waves,
That desire, that attraction
Affection we crave
Those biting lips
Restless blinks
Blushing cheeks,
Jelly knees, they're so weak
That state of bliss
Consummated by a kiss
Blows by me,
Gently as if it's a harmless breeze
Is it really so filled with ease?
In time, we'll see . . . .

STRANDED

Silence,
That's all that's left
After your bullets,
After your theft,
There's only a hole punched through
An ache that's a constant reminder of you
Eyes, just thirsting for your sight
My despair is playing tricks on my mind
I jump around and smile
But, I'm hopeless when I walk the mile
I live,
But only for the sake of it
I laugh
Only 'cuz of the irony of it
'Cuz when you were mine
I needed nothing else
Now that you're gone
I have no defense
Where'd you go?
Why did you hide?
Were you just a wave in a tide?
Questions with no answers
Just filled with regret
There are just memories and moments
Scattered in the tears that are shed.

STRANGERS

A hint of a spark,
That quick remark,
The heavy weight of the words
That hangs between us,
The shying of eyes,
The silence as cold as ice,
That seems to shatter between us
The bland fear,
Turns to salty tears
And lets the feelings show
That were sheltered within us,
We walk together
Live the moment
Remember it forever,
Until there's nothing between us,
There's nothing between us.

SVELTE

We're together, yet apart,
We're the remains,
Of love's broken heart,
We're perfect, yet too close,
You're my word; I'm your prose,
You're fire and I'm ice,
To exist, we must sacrifice,
For we burn bright,
Make a lovely sight,
Till we're shadowed by the cowardly night,
That cinches in,
All our flights,
We're warriors,
Fighting our armors,
We've ignited,
We've proved our power,
We've fought and lost,
All that had a meaning,
For that's what love is,
Beautiful, threatening and demeaning.

THE EDGE

There are a lot of questions,
I've been meaning to ask you,
A lot of words,
That I've wanted to say to you,
Some feelings, a request,
Some questions,
You'll never be able to answer,
I bet,
Some thoughts I've been wanting,
To say out loud,
Some rhymes that remain merely words,
They never turn to sounds,
Some confessions,
Actually just one,
The one that will forever remain,
On the tip of my tongue.

THE GIFT

Dreaming of moments
That will never exist,
Trying to feel the touch of your skin
Only to watch it turn to mist,
Walking down a thorny path
With my eyes shut,
That's the power of my faith
My trust,
Laughing at your little whispers,
Catching your eye
Taking a second more to linger,
Trying my best to
Make you disappear,
Wishing with all my heart
For you to still be here,
Struggling to face destiny
And let you live,
Keeping these feelings a mystery
That's the last gift
To you, I'll give.

THE SOUND

Tears, whispers
Sorrows, despair
Love, war
It's truth against lies
It's about compromise,
It's about sacrifice
It's about relations,
It's about the fights
It's about dreaming peacefully
When off go the lights,
It's about the smiles
It's about walking the mile,
It's about the kiss
That gives you a glimpse of bliss,
It's about the bearing, the sharing
It's about drifting apart,
It's about loving to go back to the start,
It's all bout this simple thing
That our world revolves around
Just look into you heart
Touch the ground,
Listen hard for a sound

THE UNSENT LETTER

Hey,
There's something I've been meaning
To say
Something that my eyes have attempted
To convey
But it's time I brought these thoughts
To my tongue
While my hair's black
And I'm still young
It's painfully simple
What I've to say
But these simple syllables
Go a long way
So I admit I've
Taken my share of time,
to let you know
To muster courage and
Let the reality show,
It's rather funny
'Cuz I've said this before,
But I think it was discreet
'Cuz you simply ignored,
This is a laughable attempt at glee
What will be the outcome
We'll just have to see,
So I'll pretty this up
And post it out,
I hope you're reply
Doesn't make me pout.

TRAGIC

Holes,
Embedded in my heart
I try to be whole,
I try my best
But the pain just sears through,
It's a constant reminder
Of my time with you,
The pain goes deep,
It finds it way into every lost memory,
And seeps,
It stiffens my body,
Freezes my heart,
It embodies my soul,
For the wrath, it's just a start,
My insides it withers,
It makes me shiver,
With chills,
Yet the feeling's so enticing,
A little bit of thrill,
Pain, I guess it's not bad,
After all, not all endings,
Can be what mine is,
Sad.

YOURS, TRULY

The world sees you,
As playing the strings of a guitar,
In reality,
You're playing the strings,
Of my heart,
You're making music of broken pieces,
Sewing them together,
All the injuries are coming to ceases,
To the world,
You're just mumbling,
In reality,
All my worries,
To sleep you're humming,
To the world,
You're just a guy with long fingers
To me,
You're the reason
A smile on my face lingers,
To the world,
I somehow belong to you,
To you,
I belong to the world,
Just an unknown girl.

LIFE

A LONELY ROAD

A screeching creek,
A silent step,
A breeze welcomes my face,
It's dangerously loud
My heart's pace,
I'm walking into darkness,
In search of light,
I'm walking alone,
To have someone by my side,
I walk in silence,
So people mark my words
I walk the long way,
So one day I can fly like a bird
I write in solace,
So one day,
My words can unite the human race
I loathe and live
A distant dream,
But maybe it's closer,
Than it seems.

C'EST LA VIE

Life, it's
So unpredictable,
Sometimes it's rough
Other time it's stable,
It twists and turns
Causes burns,
It heals, it cures
My faith in God,
It restores
It's priceless,
Yet it's overwhelming,
It's beautiful at times
Also it's a mess
It's a pain,
It's as fresh as rain
It's a boon,
It's a curse
It winds toward
Better or for worse,
It's a question
Never to be answered,
It's a complication
Never to be solved,
It's just a word
Which could mean nothing,
Or mean the world
Or just the story,
Of one unknown girl.

CLARITY

A million words,
That are left unsaid,
A violent hunger,
That's rested with a serving of lead,
A thousand sounds
That are neighbors to the wind,
One simple reason
I didn't give in,
Not to the voices,
Or the words,
For they may have allure,
But my heart, it's pure
The path's clear,
I'm creeping near,
Feeding on fear,
Shedding the last tear,
'Till the skies clear
'Cuz I'm here

CREST

Shallow waters,
Deep with souls,
Everything that matters
Is embedded in the body as a whole,
All that's forgotten
Is the bed of the sea,
All that's hoped for
Is the water in its entirety,
Things we cherish
Wash over like waves,
Things we crave
Are simple corals,
Left on the beach to save,
Time is the flow,
Which demeans us all,
Life is a mystery,
Or so is called.

DIVE

L ife, Death
Truth and lies,
The bittersweet reality
Of sacrifice,
Music, dance
The first start,
The soft thud of my heart
That whisper of love,
That sword of youth
It wrinkles the
Soft veil of truth,
The miracle of every breath,
The taste of salty death,
A flap of time's wings
So solemnly, the bells like
Words ring,
The beauty of it all
Sinks in,
In life's skin and bone
I'm diving in.

DREAMS

Dreams, hope
Colors, love
The desire to break free of responsibilities
And fly off like a dove,
To enjoy and dance
To sing in the rain,
Those were things of happiness in the past,
It's amazing how fast things change,
Suddenly all I have is duties,
Which I oblige to gleefully,
All I want is to be stable,
And keep my feet on the ground
With my mind's guidance,
As the only sound
I just want to be sane,
To work for gain
And just be ordinary,
Rather than losing myself
In the race to be extraordinary.

DROPS

Raindrops fall on my window
I'm watching them race,
They bring a smile to my face,
I watch them slide
On the glass they glide,
Is that how my life will be?
Have I been sent to Earth,
To battle it out
For God's entertainment and glee?
The drops fall
And wash away the tears,
Am I just one of these drops
Lost in life's crosshairs?
Am I just a faint sound
Or am I a scream?
Is there any meaning
Behind the dreams I dream?
Am I just a carrier of a season
Sent down for seemingly no reason?
Am I here with my antics
Just to enchant
So when I fall down
Everyone will be racing to dance on my heart?
Am I just a girl
lost in this world?
Even though a raindrop's life is a tragedy
it's a drop not a girl I'd rather be.

ETRANGER

Loneliness,
It always seemed like
A stranger,
It was the enemy
I was the fighting ranger,
Until suddenly,
My energy died out
And loneliness housed in me,
I didn't see anyone around
It felt so different,
So at peace
Every word muttered by my heart,
I could hear with ease,
Every crowd,
Seemed to disappear,
Suddenly I needed no one near,
Surprisingly, it wasn't a curse,
It was the people, who were worse,
It felt so serene,
Just my soul and me
To feel free,
To be solitary,
To be the hero of my story
To bask in my own glory,
And shine
To make up for all the wasted time
And discover the hidden me,
The reality, of what could be.

FADE AWAY!

A color splashed on a canvas,
That makes the whiteness fade away,
A candlelight,
That fades the darkness away,
A whisper
That fades the silence away,
If small things, can make
Things so big disappear
After death
Will I fade away?
Will I be a loner soul
Left astray?
Will I just vanish
In thin air?
Will it be like
I wasn't even there?
I'm curious to know
The fear's beginning to grow,
I don't want to
Be lifted away,
I don't want to
Go the silent way,
I don't want to fade away!

FLOW

Friendship,
Does it really last?
Time,
Why does it fly by so fast?
Hope,
It flickers like a candlelight
Dreams,
They become nightmares
And haunt me at night
Silence,
It's what's left after the violence
Scars,
Serve as reminders of the war
They go deeper every hour
Love,
It lays flightless
Like an injured dove
Words,
They seem to fade away,
Never to see the light of day,
This poem,
It flows till it ends
So long my friends.

FRIENDSHIP

F riendship is so beautiful
  So pure
Ever wound, every scar
It can cure
Friendship is the feeling
We all cherish
Without which
We would all perish,
It's the sunshine
On a stormy day
It's the one thing
For which I pray
It's not something you buy
It's something you earn
Through the course of it's dwindling path
Lessons you learn
It's as pretty as can be
It fills our heart with glee
I wonder how it would feel
It would be surreal
It's the first and last thing
I want to feel
I wish friendship was real.

GO ON!

Tears fall down on the ground,
Everything's absolutely still
There's no sound,
Her life is flowing away like a waterfall
There's nothing that matters
There's no one to call,
Her eyes look down
As her lips pull up a painful frown
Can't look up
She can't face this brutal world,
A lonely girl
She has to struggle
Through all her plans,
She will have to muddle
She will have to bleed
In this game of life
She will never lead,
For victory, she will have to plead
Yet she suffers
She walks on this unpaved road,
'Cuz she has to move on
On this terrible road of life
She will have to go on
'Cuz she knows that one day she will make it,
To the top,
From there?
She'll never drop.

GROW BACK DOWN

Remember the times
When we would pout
For a bit of candy
When life was 'hide and seek'
And everything was dandy
When friendship
Was molded out of laughter
And a little 'Play-Doh'
When everything was so new
When it was only the channel number
Of 'Disney' we needed to know,
When we wore little frocks
And shoes that would light up
Oh! How I wish
We'd never grown up.

GROWING UP

Sunlight warms my feet,
My heart rejoices as it
Flies to the rhythm of its beat
It soars up above in the sky
All my dreams
Are beginning to fly,
All my visions
Are turning to reality,
All my aspirations
Are coming closer to sanity,
All the lessons I've learned
Are coming to use,
Wisdom, emotions and logic
Are beginning to fuse,
For I'm growing up
Becoming mature
I've learned how to heal
And how to cure,
The world seemed a mystery
It's not anymore,
'Cuz it seems like I've found my place
Where I'm accepted
And I'm beautiful and filled with grace
I've found my path,
Found my way
I'm finally not just another teen astray.

HEAVEN AND HELL

Tears, whispers
Life, death
Songs, emotions
a tear to shed,
Laughter, ecstasy
The glistening of eyes,
Turmoil, thunder
Taken by surprise,
A heartfelt kiss
A heart-breaking goodbye,
The glimpse of heaven
The living in hell
Remembering the rise
And the grave where the drops fell,
Writing, reciting
Humoring, screaming
These are the things that I live for
The things that make me want to quit trying.

HOST

Life and death,
Are defined
By just a single breath,
But love and sorrow,
They ignite
The hollow bodies we host,
They beautify,
And glorify
The past's hidden ghosts,
They turn dust to tears,
Taste to fears,
A someone to a 'dear'
They define and undermine,
The reality of who we could be
The life of a wonder,
The shallow human being.

HUES

Faint calls of home,
They echo in the soul
The lost fragrance in the air,
Was my only way back home
The soft greeting of drops,
Is met with tears of my own
For after years of wearing a mask,
My withered beauty, I've finally shown
My weakened eyes are searching
For the painter of the skies,
My shattered spirit is clearing
The truth from the lies,
My treacherous love is lurking
In the shadows of my youth,
While my entire being is drained,
Of the creator's beautiful hues.

IMAGINERS

There is a darkness,
Clouding my eyes
There is a thirst in my heart,
That yearns for light
There is a part of me,
That wonders why
I was the one
Chosen to be blind,
It's not as sad as people imagine it to be,
It's like living in another world
A world made for those like me,
It's where I imagine
How things would be,
How the world would look like
If I could see,
It's where I wonder
What must be the exact shade of blue
Of the sky,
It's where I wonder
How people look like, when they lie,
It's where imaginers like me
Feel strong,
It's where I feel I belong
It's this darkness
That identifies me
And sets my imagination free
But even though I'm happy
With this world of my own
I wish it was your world I could see.

LIGHTS OUT

There's a peace found,
When one falls to the ground
There's a light that surrounds,
It wills us to complete,
The final rounds,
There's a voice that beholds,
The owner, well He's just a mould,
There's a flash
Of blurs and truth,
The montage, of youth
A crack, in the kingdom of love,
A track, that takes one high above
A low whisper
A silent quiver,
The end,
Never differs.

MACABRE

Skin, that's striped,
That's marked with scars,
Hands that house strength,
A will that holds power,
A voice that upholds,
The warrior's honor
A quest that beholds,
The rust to my armor
A mind that echoes
The calls of war
Humanity, that's surrendered to foes,
It grows fainter every hour,
A life that renders useless,
Like the bullets I discard,
Raise your glasses for the cruelty,
For the triumph,
Of the Devil's hour.

MY JOURNEY

A long winding road,
A graveled path
Grass as soft as that of a meadow,
Is that where my journey starts?
Is it the wet air of the ocean
Or the musk scent of trees?
Or is it a busy city,
Where pollution replaces the breeze?
Is it in the loving comfort
Of a mother's hug,
Or it walking streets discreetly,
At the hideout of thugs?
Is it at the foothill of a climb
Ready to surmount,
Or is it the yard of my house
Where I'll be sent away by the music of wind chimes?
Or is it these words
Which have come to define
My small little world?
Or is it welcomed by the sun?
Well, all I know is,
My journey's begun.

PEOPLE PUZZLE

B eautiful people,
With the noblest of hearts
Scared people,
With traces of dark
Sunny people,
With absolutely no care
Weary people,
Who just want to believe God's there
Soulful people who make you smile
Hurt people who tread the miles
I wonder how a species
Could be so alike yet, so different
A race so rash,
Yet the participants so vibrant,
I wonder how many personalities
Does the world 'people' cover?
But it's through the course of life
These puzzles we discover,
Their answers we uncover.

REALM

D ragged through the borders
Of heaven and hell,
Happiness lies in which realm
Who can tell,
Where does my soul
Truly belong,
Where can I be a whole
And keep my heart strong,
Where can I feel passion
A fire, burn inside,
Where can all my memories
And ashes reside,
Where does bliss lie,
Answering these questions.
Seems vain even to try,
So I'll just lay here
And melt away my youth,
My tears, my blood
Will show me the route.

STILLS

Thoughts,
That's what life is,
Thinking about the future
Thinking about all the things you missed,
Pondering at the sight
Of an old lover,
Racking your brain
Trying to find cover,
Remembering moments that have long gone by
Holding on to something that's lost,
But you still try,
Laughing at a glimpse of the glory times,
Finding peace in the faint music of chimes,
Mouthing the words, you've always wanted to say,
Reminiscing the choices
Did you choose the right way?
Lost in the echoes,
The whispers of time
Stills that will be forever yours,
Forever mine.

SWEET SUCCESS

Innocence,
the presence of simple brilliance
is that what it takes to survive?
Or is it fighting hard
breaking hearts
That makes one strive?
Is it smiling along the way,
or making life's actions grey
that paves the way to success?
Is it ignorance
or a caring presence
that makes you someone,
or is it staying in the shadows,
that gets you there?
Is it dignity,
or beauty
or is it abiding by duty?
Is it a challenge
or a hassle to manage,
is it something I can achieve?
Or is it just another lie
that we're all forced to believe?

SWORDS

If I ever could
Make happiness simply mine
If I could sit back and just watch
The flying time,
If I could just be where I stand,
The place where fear seems a bit distant
And a pen remains clasped in my hand,
If I could freely take off
And just fly away,
If I could be up in the sky
And still stay,
Frozen in time, frozen in thoughts
I wonder why I get lost in delusions
And tie myself in knots,
For life may be rough,
And it may be unfair,
But I have to keep fighting
And keep my heart there,
So if all these demands,
Don't come true,
I won't back down,
I won't fall through
I'll simply be making my way
Up to the top,
For once I start the war
It'll never stop,
The sword of courage in my hands
Will never drop

THE BOAT

The river flows on,
     As the boat rows along
The sun shines
As the boat gracefully sways
Then comes the light evening
When another boat comes in the way
Then descends the night,
With it's dreadful fright,
When the river starts tumbling
Making the boat rock,
It's journey
The boat wants to stop,
Then comes the dawn
When darkness fades away,
When everything seems blissful
The boat's finally got its way,
As it reaches up in heaven
For forever in time,
But the river still flows
Flows, like the Lord divine

UNITY IN DESPAIR

Blood on the ground,
There is only rage
The heart doesn't make a sound,
Sulphur hangs in the air
Bullets are flying everywhere
That simple guy
Ever so shy,
Is bullied by stronger men
He tries to fight back,
They force him to give in
The lady with her face covered
Fights the man in the muslin cloth,
For her right, her freedom
For they're all she's got
That addict enclosed in a cell
Fights his temptation to get well,
That lady who lost custody of her child
Fights her alcoholic husband,
To protect her child,
The man who was fired
For being detected with a disease,
Fights with the stereotypical mindsets
In return, to only be teased,

Everyone, everywhere
Fights a war
Fights a battle of right against wrong
Doesn't back down, remain strong,
For life may be hard, it may be tough
But we have to stand up and say "that's enough",
And fight for the right
And win the fight against people,
Against life.

UNSUNG

It's funny
How life is strange,
It twists and turns
Until it leaves you deranged,
It slips and slides
My strength it undermines
Why does it have to be so hard
Why does it always have to be
About the one who survives?
What about the soldier
Who dies on the field?
What about the broken heart,
Whose soul was revealed
What about the man
Who was happy to face death
What about the lady, who sacrificed herself
For a baby's first breath?
What about the poet
Who remained a secret till her words spread?
What about those,
Who are dead?
What about the strugglers?
The 'sidies' in the story
Where is their fame
Where is their glory?

WEAPONLESS WAR

L ife is a constant war,
Sometimes against friends
Just trying to make amends,
Sometimes against death
Just trying to catch hold of that last breath,
Sometimes, against love
Simply trying to fly off like a dove,
Sometimes against the world
The entire world against one girl,
a girl caught up in tangles
Who sees life from different angles
a girl who fights wars with herself
She's clueless about the consequences,
Or about the end
She's simply trying to fight all these wars,
Without wearing out
She's only aiming that out of these wars,
Victorious she'll come out.

WHY?

Have you ever wondered
If life is fair
Is God even up there?
Why can't we see the breeze?
Why we shut our eyes when we sneeze
Why girls repel boys
Why children love new toys
Why we don't nurture imagination
Why we don't encourage creation
Why are we scared of people's thoughts?
Why in problem, we tie ourselves in knots
Why we try to be someone else
Why we always try to impress
Why we always want to fashion a cool dress
Why can't life be simple?
Why can't every girl have dimples?
Why can't we fly?
What would happen if we tried?
I wonder why so many questions
Take shelter in my heart
I want to find the answers
But where to start
Am I to discover myself or answer this puzzle?
But right now
I just want to live
'Cuz I know through the course of life
I'll figure out the answers
When the time is right.

LOSS

BEAUTIFUL CURSE

Tears that trickle
Down her rosy cheeks,
Sorrow that makes her more beautiful
Despair that makes her insides weak,
Curls that highlight her eyes
Locks that hide the tears she cries,
Lips that make people thirst
Wounds that make her condition worse,
Hands so soft, yet untouched
Hands that scar and hurt much,
Ears dressed in priceless pearls
Beauty dressed
In the demands of the world
This is the story of every girl,
Existing in the brutal world.

CONFESSIONS

Silence,
It's the easiest act of violence,
For it spreads darkness
It overshadows might,
It with its magnificent power,
Veils the sound of one's yelps and plights,
It ends all laughter
It shuns the three words,
That make 'happily ever after',
It disconnects you from the world,
It puts your head in a swirl,
'Cuz in it's cover,
You're forced to surrender,
Give in to your aches
And just slip under,
Somewhere so down below,
It's impossible to break free,
Where the hidden despair of blackness,
Darkens every gleeful memory,
Where your soul gets crushed,
Into nothing,
But bits of dust.

CONFLICTED

Sitting inquisitively
Pondering at the mysteries
That are all around,
I sit quietly
But my heart's flooded with sounds,
I feel invisible
As if I'm walking Death's haunting pace
No music, no words
Have the grace
To convey,
What my harrowing soul wants to say,
They think silence is something of wisdom
In reality,
It's just the entrance to loneliness's kingdom
I wonder and write,
About a life
That seems to be his,
But may just become mine.

CRIMSON

B its and pieces,
Lie on the floor
I walk on them barefoot,
Just to see if I could
Bear any more pain,
To see if I can escape the numbness
And feel again,
I smile at the river of red
'set me free' the pain said,
so I did
the jar of tears I'd hidden
I opened its lid,
And watched as the river's
Color faded,
To the land of angels
I had finally made it.

DECEPTION

A thirst for glee,
A reason to be
If only they could be seen,
The notes written for this melody,
A longing for a first,
An emptiness, that ceases to burst
A truth that struggles to shine,
A destiny,
That awaits to be mine,
A hope,
That wants to believe,
A breath
That wants to relieve,
A soul
That aches to retrieve,
What can never be achieved.

DISCONNECT

Love or hate
Is that one's fate?
To be drowned in
Seas of tears
Or be the reason
Of everyone's cheers
Is there such a clear divide?
Between who to respect
And who to banish from one's heart and mind?
Is it so simple?
'Cuz in my world
These things are just a swirl
Is love really true?
Or could it just be
One of my hundred dreams
Associated with you
Is smiling even a cure
I thought it was,
But I don't know anymore
I thought I was
Loved and adored
Now suddenly, I feel lonely
It's like of me, people just got bored
I feel like I'm drowning
In my own little world of pain
a place, where no one knows my name

Where I can simply
Let go of all relations
And get rid of my heart's complications
And be greedy,
And selfish
It's better than to be
An angel for the world
And still feel hellish
It's better than to watch
My own soul perish.

DIVINATION

Fear of the future,
That invokes the darkness buried in,
A threat of falling,
That imposes the task of committing a sin,
A dark force calling,
It breaks through my hard skin,
I'm letting go
It's the aroma of death, I'm breathing in,
Courage is rendered useless
For the devil feeds on its kin,
Fighting is senseless,
For the war's fought within,
It's a game full of lies,
When it comes to torture,
There's no compromise,
Just hold onto your soul,
Until it flies,
The tears of a painful end,
It cries.

DOWN BELOW

Disappointment in myself,
By regret I'm overwhelmed,
How could things have gone so far,
I'm unable to escape,
I'm stuck in fear's jar
Why has the fear,
Seem to have won,
How did it win the war,
When did its realm begin
It makes it so hard to fight,
It's like I'm committing a sin
It's darkness shadows,
My every move
Its echo blackens,
And blurs the truth,
It covers me in the night
Of my own will,
I'll keep drowning
Unless I try to break through,
But till then,
I'm stuck in my nightmares of you.

EASE

T houghts flow freely,
　 I sit in solace
As in my mind
Thousands of memories race
They form a blur
As I try to clear
All my apprehensions, all my fears
I think of happiness
It makes me grin
I think of every committed sin
I think of death,
Of every single breath
I think of deceit
I think of all the hurdles
I've had to greet
I think of life,
Just a blink of an eye
As I let out a sigh
For I'm lost
I'm tied in knots
By regret, greed and pain
I wonder why
I put myself through this everyday,
I wait for my heart to answer,
It has nothing to say,
I'm just another girl gone astray
But still everyday I reminisce,
I think,
'Cuz that's what life is
Sorrow, memories and a quill.

FRENEMIES

These days
It seems like my friends and I
Have parted ways,
It's like we're
Black and white,
I'm always wrong
They're always right
It gives me such a fright,
It's like we're completely different,
Our friendship's dead
The same which once felt effervescent,
I guess it's just a lesson
To learn how to let go
It's a tough ride,
God knows
I wonder why we bother with friendship
If it never lasts
Why do we take a chance?
Why do we walk to our own doom
To feel alone, in a crowded room
I thought I had found
'true' friends
but I'm just left with a broken heart
and shattered dreams
but that's how the story,
always ends.

GODLY GRIP

I stand alone,
In a crowded room
It's full of noise and laughter,
While I'm bathed in gloom
Everyone's celebrating
For one reason or the other,
While I'm forced to silently witness
My soul wither,
They're glowing and shining,
I'm undermining,
They're smiling and talking,
The road of life
Alone I'm walking,
Why?
Is there some pain or meaning,
Hidden in the words I cry?
Is this numbness
Here for a reason,
Or is it just a visitor
Like a season,
Whatever it may be,
The power to get me through,
Lies in the soft hands,
Of the firm you.

HIDDEN

Streaming sunlight
Thirsty lips,
They wish to speak
But they're jinxed,
Words that hope to touch,
Cheeks that wish to blush,
A veil that wants to be lifted,
An expression that wants to be shifted,
A truth that aches to reveal,
A conscience that struggles to conceal,
A war that wants to be consummated,
A peace sign that needs to be obliterated,
A simple journey
That seems to be winding too far,
It grows deeper and darker
Every hour,
It twists and turns
Until the light,
Breaks another dream,
Belonging to the night.

I'VE GOT IT

Tears fall on the floor
Just falling, wasting there
I'm having a private moment,
Why does everybody else in the room have to stare?
Why can't I stop the water from flowing?
It's like the pain's growing
And I'm slowing,
I don't want to be the weakling
Who simply cries,
Just gives up
Before she tries,
I don't want to be the coward,
I don't want to be afraid,
Cuz I'm not
And it's fine if I've got nothing
At least honor I've got
At least courage I've got.

IGNITION

Moments of truth,
Flashes of flight,
The wars we've fought
And won to survive,
Thunders of blackness,
Fits of madness
We've seen,
Things that erase,
The faint calls of who we'd been,
Hanging Sulphur,
Tangles of weariness trace the air,
The burnt road,
Screams, life isn't fair,
We've known it all along,
But we've remained strong
And lost our souls in the wager,
For matters of the heart,
They just add fuel to the danger

INIQUITOUS

Dark nights
Bright lights,
Flowers bloom
As they lie on graves gloom,
The stars happily shine
As she sits under them and undermines,
The ring on her hand glitters
But her days are bitter,
She lived in wrath
Not knowing the aftermath,
She never was benign
Or the girl with the charm
She was a flower
Or her journey was such
She started as a bud
And bloomed slowly
And attracted all sorts of things to her knowingly,
Until the day came,
When the bloom started washing away
Each petal just blackening and wasting away,
Until there was nothing left
But a colorless stem
What about her friends,
She just left them

There was nothing left to say
Everything was just black and grey
She wanted to be left astray,
And just sit in solace
Dreaming of that place
She knew so well,
All the hatred that took shelter in her heart
Broke out and tore her apart,
Suddenly her eyes went red
She wanted to be dead
She grabbed that razor
Cackled, cut herself
And let the vivid red blood out
As the light went out of her eyes
And came out a devil
Who took her soul,
And floated to hell.

MIST

Dew drops race down the window,
I lie wide-awake on my pillow,
Tears sweep down,
The face in the mirror
Always seems to wear a frown,
The wind blows in silently,
I sit up
My body shakes violently,
There's a secret inside the moves
I seem to be stuck up,
In the past's grooves
Sometimes, the day seems to be hope
Sometimes, it seems like another end
To all those efforts I made to cope,
With my loss, my pain
It's like a constant strain
But I still wake,
My eyes do run dry
I think I can take it
If I use all my might,
I will survive
In the pain and sorrow
I will not dive.

PUPPETEER

Shadows,
They tower over my past,
Intimidating and tall,
Their darkness leaves me aghast,
They don't leave my side,
They're hitched with me,
It's a long ride,
They remain unseen,
When a smile,
Dares to erase what's been,
They thunder on my skies,
When rain escapes,
My cloudy eyes,
They burn into the spirit,
They choke on my will,
They haunt every moment,
They own the quill.

RAGE

Anger pulses,
Down my fragile veins,
The withheld anger and wrath,
Comes out
Easing the strain,
The blood gushes,
And fights the war against the heat,
There's violence,
A rage hidden in the beat,
There's growls and weapons,
Made of pure vengeance
My thoughts are clouded,
By a Sulphur haze,
There's a devil dancing,
Igniting the craze,
There's a longing, a thirst,
His throat, I want to burst
Into a million pieces,
Until all that's left is a head,
Tattered remains, and a conscience,
Full of creases.

REASONABLE DISTANCE

We're distant
Like the sky and the sea,
We're what people think about
When they think of
What may never be,
I had wanted to change
But deep down had accepted fate,
Until you changed the entire look
You're reach to me
Made me believe we're something out of a book,
You're changing moods
Two faced words
Began to intrude
Into everything I was,
And what was in me
Your ability to change me
Made me realize,
No matter how tough I may act
I'm still a 'she'
It was confusing and tangled
Our little issue
But I'm done searching for peace
in the roller coaster ride, that is you.

REDEMPTION

Flashes flicker
 Nightmares snicker,
As they haunt my lonely world,
Lightening thunders
I'm paying for all the blunders,
Forces fighting to kill a girl,
Clouds roll on,
The rain grows strong
As it gives my soul a whirl,
The wind screams,
The devil gleams
As he looks down at his prized pearl,
Visions shatter,
Teary eyed gather,
To mourn the death of the girl,
Who paid the price,
For loving the world.

ROYALS

Loneliness,
It creeps like vines
It twists and turns
All my fears it intertwines,
It holds me in
And breaks my will,
It tries to separate,
My soul from my quill,
It seizes and captures
Every whispered word,
It hunts and renders flightless
Every hopeful bird,
It casts a shadow,
Over every ray of sunshine
It steals away my virtues,
Those, which are rightfully, mine
It crawls on my back
It brings me down,
It will always linger
And tag my head,
Like a crown.

SAVE ME!

Sometimes, I feel lost
Lost and scared,
Scared about the future
Crying over the past,
But most of all
Terrified from the creature
Growing inside my heart,
It's like poison
Mixed in wine,
Beautiful when given in
And horrendous when out
It's changing me,
Into something I'm not,
It's turning me into someone else
Drowning my conscience
Making it useless,
It's reigning me in
Somebody help me!
Untie these knots
Save me from the Devil,
Save me from God,
Save me from committing a sin
Just save me from dying within
Save, at least what's left,
Someone please save me
Save me from myself.

SILHOUETTE

A closing silhouette,
A long overdue debt,
A quiet, that's outgrown its time,
A serenity, that's lost its shine
A truth, that's lost its youth
Feelings, that are weary of being mute
A distance that was once seen
Has given way, for intimacy to be revealed,
A joy, that's one to be reveled,
Shadows that are no longer disheveled,
A past traced by horror,
A memoir kept for honor,
A longing, triumphed by pride
Widowed by darkness,
Soon to be bride.

SINKING

Life is filled with sorrow,
There's nothing to expect from tomorrow,
There's nothing to dream about
Nothing to scream about,
Nothing to live for
It's as if I'm disconnected
From this very Earth,
Where everyone takes birth
I want to die,
I want to let the emptiness out
With the tears I cry,
I want to stay in here forever
And stay cold,
It's like somebody sucked out the very life out of me
It's like I have eyes urging to open,
With nothing to see,
It's like I'm sinking to the bottom of the ocean
Not gasping for air,
But waiting to hit the rocks
Where I can get rid of these thoughts.

THE END

My hand clenches,
As it tries to hold on to the past
But, it's time to let go,
Nothing's ever built to last
It hurts to let go
When will the pain ease?
Does anyone know?
Memories flash by
And cloud my eyes,
It's like they're devils
In angelic disguise
I'm drowning,
At my weakened will
My heart is frowning,
But, alas there's no other choice
No escape
There's just surrendering to the noise
More of this fighting, I can't take,
There's just whispering
My last words of goodbye,
There's just waiting for the end to come
As time passes by

THORNS

A kingdom of blackness,
Is the address of thee,
The only way to reach it,
Is to wash away my glee,
The track that gives it away,
Doesn't even house,
A dog that's astray,
The feet that have acquainted your grounds,
The dust never heard again,
Their sounds,
The directions,
They're simple,
Just walk, feel and burn,
For the kingdom of treachery,
Is just one wrong turn.

TREACHEROUS

Contentment,
A word that fulfills it's meaning,
Only when I'm with you,
Love, desire, faith
It's your presence,
That makes them true,
Hope, risk, fate,
The ability to intake,
The pain and the stakes,
Is a resistance which only you,
Can make,
For you are not a dream,
You're not a lie,
You're the reality,
You've caught my eye,
You're not a passerby; you'll stay,
You're my only chance,
To make his memories fade away.

TRULY ME

Silence,
That's what I need
To get back from 'fake wannabe'
To being simply me,
Distance from all the
Superficial desires,
To enjoy in peace
The singing of my heart's choir,
Abandonment
From all the enemies,
So I can allow the
Hate clouding my eyes, to drift off
And see clearly
A break-up
From all the fake relations,
A break
From life and its complications,
A deep breath
To blow away my regrets,
A tear
To take away the pain,
And make it flow away, all that fear
A loose end,
Some time for it to mend
These are my needs,
To be more than an image
To be truly me.

UNFOUND

Entangled in the nets of time,
Lost in the echoes
Of voices that were once mine,
Helpless in the twists
And turns of this life,
Cut by the edges
Of betrayal, they're as sharp as knives
Hopeless in despair,
To close to the truth to dare,
To lost to call for aid,
To late to change my mind
The decision's made,
The fight's lost
My time is gone,
All that's left
Is a simple song.

US

A word,
That turns into foggy breath,
A desire,
That leads to death,
Desperation,
That left us cold,
The pain,
It never gets old,
The journey, it's endless,
Me? I'm left breathless,
Heart's surrendered,
While my will blindly looks on,
As if these pain
Will turn into a song,
As if we were meant to be,
All along,
As if we're one,
As if the world houses,
You, me and none,
As if these words,
Are a distant dream,
A nightmare,
The future's scream.

EVERYTHING

ELSE . . .

ALLUME

Lights that soar,
And greet the sky,
They reflect on my window,
They shine in my eye,
They float on the water,
As it ripples their path,
They illuminate the track,
For every dream I've ever hath,
They shimmer in glory,
Every flicker sings a story.

BLASPHEMY

That static hair,
  Those deadly glares,
Those sinful treats,
The continuous beat,
Those crumbled feet,
Long journeys under the heat,
The endless sand,
A one-man band,
Passing through the trees,
Trees stripped bare,
The man's closet stripped of care,
His rugged hands,
Birth poetry and prose,
The passion igniting his hands,
Worked his toes,
For he walks and walks,
With only a soul to mock
His tryst with destiny,
His final stand,
of blasphemy.

BLINDED

Had I known
That when I rose,
At me stones would've been thrown
I'd have screamed
Had I known
That when I grow
The true colors of people I'd know,
I'd rise,
Had I known
That when I love,
I'd be broken down
I'd never let my love go unrequited
I'd fight and tackle,
I'd win every battle,
I'd conquer,
I'd thrive,
Every struggle
I'd survive,
I'd be free
Of all the regrets of being blinded,
By fantasies of glee.

BRIGHT LIGHT

A little joke,
That brightens your day
A tedious job,
That can be turned to play
Burst out laughing,
Scream with joy
All the moments in life
You must enjoy,
Open your heart
For starters,
Make friends
Then try a little harder,
Speak out loud
Face a crowd,
Be daring
Have the devil inside you to dare,
Don't let wimpy people give you a scare,
Just live like a king
To your hearts content sing,
Know that you can do it
Just smile,
There's nothing to it.

BUS BACK HOME

Roads, paths
The traffic overpowers
The sound of my beating heart,
The roar of the bus
It's tilting every second
Is a must
The windows are shaking
Laughter's breaking
Free from the lips of two little girls,
Oh! How simple is their world,
We drive by a house and I see
A child begging on the street
I wonder how does his family
Make ends meet?
We stop at a temple
A little prayer I mumble
We reach a busy market
Full of shops
I'm wondering what's the next stop
I sit silently
Looking out
When fate confirms my doubt,
My stop was here
It was a land full of cheer
So I got down,
And looked behind
As I realized
I had just left that heaven
That everybody tries to find.

DARKNESS

Black ink spreads
On a white page,
Ashes take place of fire
That once lit up with rage
The night for instance,
Takes place of the sun's brilliance
Why is that darkness,
Is said to conquer light?
Why is it said to be a dreadful sight?
When it is in darkness
That our mind finds solace
And dreams,
It is in the blackness
That the struggling soul is forced to scream,
It is in the stillness
Where the most beautiful sounds are heard,
It is when words
Of togetherness are uttered
Darkness is not a fright;
It is a power,
That need not show it's might
It is misunderstood
Its capabilities are feared,
Just like the girl
Who's writing these words here.

FEELINGS

Feelings,
    They come and go,
Some stay sheltered in our hearts,
While others compete to show
Feelings,
Every minute they grow
The root cause of them,
Is difficult to know
They're just a symphony,
Flowing continuously through our heart
Notes so powerful,
There is no end, just a start
Voices whispering softly,
Lingering in our minds
Trying to intertwine
With logic of the brain,
It's really strange
They're the symbols of our character
A painting of our souls
It's their wrath,
That can leave a hole,
It's their bonds
Which make us realize
Who we are and who we can be,
Oh! If only the true form of my feelings
I could see.

FICTITIOUS

Beauty,
Bowing down to it
Has become a duty,
It's become vain,
To try and win the game
Against those battering eyelashes,
And blond curls
Beauty dressed
In the evils of the world,
Beauty that remains ever thyne
There's no shimmering ray of hope,
That can make it mine
Beauty so true,
Twisted in lies
I lay in wait,
For this 'beauty' to die.

FIRST

The strings of that old guitar,
Pictures of who I used to be
That torn journal,
With a record of every hour
A recollection of that silly girl in plaits
That girl I used to call 'me'
That old and forgotten dress,
With the pink frills
That tooth hidden for the tooth fairy
Oh, hiding it was such a thrill!
That first day in school,
The time when being yourself
Was the only rule,
That best friend
Who eventually broke away in the end,
That first sleepover
Telling ghost stories under the cover,
That first game of truth and dare
The taste of cheating, being unfair
The first crush,
That shy blush,
That first book
That aggressive look,
That first taste,
That first touch
I miss very much.

FULFILLMENT

The taste of admiration,
  It's such a . . . distant sensation,
It's another page,
Another prize away,
It's another moral,
Another principal left astray,
It's a state of surrounded deceit,
It's the foreplay,
To the inevitable defeat,
It's being 'someone',
Only to lose oneself in the crowd,
It's smiling, while receiving a crown,
Only to feel its might and power,
Bury you down,
It's the sound of 'hurrahs',
Drown the reality,
Of who you are,
It's the destination,
We all want to reach,
Only to taste,
Learn and preach.

HAUNTED

Haunted by memories,
Haunted by thought,
Haunted by that little lie,
A lie that took all I had got,
Haunted by a secret,
Haunted by a whisper,
Haunted by the remains,
Of my happiness,
That still lingers,
Lost in the darkness,
Afraid of the light,
Drowning in despair,
But sinking like it's a flight,
Screaming in terror,
But the words are mute,
My body has tremors,
It shakes to the rhythm of the flute,
War rages on,
Like a never ending song,
And I just flow along,
I just flow along

INVOCATION

The reckless laughter,
Of care free souls,
The stretching smiles,
Of happy wholes,
The joyful melody,
Of chattering voices,
The gleaming auras,
Of those for whom,
Happiness is a choice,
The beautiful times,
That are created by grins,
The memories that last,
For as long as that good old joke,
The feeling of ecstasy,
We can never invoke.

MIRAGE

The sun shines and warms me,
The birds sing and call to me,
Am I just dreaming?
or is my existence finding a meaning?
Everything seems brighter,
The burdens of my heart,
Seem to be lighter,
Is it a mirage,
Or happiness in its true form,
Am I just humoring my heart's that's worn,
Time seems to fly by,
Dusk greets the magnificent sky,
Is it true,
Is it not,
Is it just a faint thought,
All I know, is one day it will pass,
time, it never lasts.

NATURE'S ARM

Twinkling lights,
   Scattered in the black sky
It's feels so perfect
It feels so right,
To be bathed in the glimmering moonlight
Trying not to shiver
As the cool breeze tickles me
It takes all my might,
But it's such a little price to pay
To feel like this, to always stay
Untouched and calm
To feel like I'm nestled
In nature's arm,
To feel the innocence
Breaking free,
To let all your worries
Flow away with the breeze,
I wish I could stay here forever
Me and silence together,
But every dream comes to an end
So I bid goodbye to you
My friend!

QUILLED

Writing,
Everything it brightens,
The burden of my heart,
With each word,
It lightens,
It lets the tears shine,
And makes you feel,
The pain that was once mine,
It gives color to a page,
Color to my life,
It reveals the truth,
Hidden in twisted lies,
A simple line,
A pleasant surprise,
It's the safe haven,
Where my feelings reside,
It washes over,
Like a tide,
If only to erode the words,
And to forever hide.

QUIVER OF QUILLS

Hunting,
It's a game of thrill,
It's the action form,
Of writing with a quill,
For when we hunt,
We take a life,
And watch the prey's light drown out,
And when we write,
A word acts like a bite
And kills all form of doubt,
When one hunts,
He is taken over
By thirst,
Like when one writes,
He is taken over
By his inner soul's plight,
When one hunts
He is taken over by rage,
An adjective that could describe
All the content on this page,

When one hunts
The prey does not die alone,
It takes with him a part of the hunter's soul
A bit of his pain, a sliver of his conscience
A bit of humanity
Every hunt becomes more obnoxious,
Just like when one writes
He leaves behind his sorrows,
A bit of his heart in every line
The hunter dies playing his own game
With no one
Who knows his name,
But a writer, well,
These words for him are untrue
As he seeks out for help
Like I seek help from you,
And yet he dies
Haunted by his own thoughts,
Just because a reader like you,
Read and forgot.

SECRETS

Life is an unspoken threat,
It haunts and lingers on,
Every word I've said,
It burdens and crushes,
It tears apart,
Every dream, every nightmare
Sheltered in my heart,
It knows all my secrets,
The harrowing truths,
Those naïve pictures I painted,
Through the course of my youth,
Those lonely nights,
Those unheard plights,
That era, that time,
Is simply another poem,
Another line.

SENSES

Desires that ache,
All the defenses,
Are beginning to break,
The notes that
Awaken the slumbered soul,
The symphony,
That completes and makes one whole,
A yearning for its touch,
It's feel,
To have it's beauty robe me,
And make impossibility,
Real.

SHRINE

There is a shrine out there,
  Simply standing in despair,
As the night gave into twilight,
The shrine just stood there,
Faking might,
It stood out,
I just kept gazing,
And read a prayer out loud,
It seemed so different,
So distant,
Yet so close to my heart,
It had enchanted me,
From the start,
As it struggled to blend into the scenery,
Even trying was vain,
It looked like the gateway to bliss,
Where He would fly to us, his kiss,
It looked majestic,
With the spectrum of the sky,
None could ignore its presence,
It's beautiful lie,
I wished to experience it
Lay under the dome
And ponder,
But then I wonder,
Why shatter the image,
Painted in my mind,
For it was enough,
To connect me to the Lord divine.

THAT SMILE . . . .

One sunny smile,
A monstrous laugh,
A sly wink of the eye,
The blushing of cheeks,
When you break a smile shy,
That evil sound,
That breaks through the teeth,
The fake smile we wear,
When family and relatives we greet,
The teary-eyed smile,
The contagious smile,
That helps us walk the mile,
It's a thing as small as can be,
Yet it fills our hearts with glee,
And it makes a more beautiful thee,
So keep smiling,
And be truly you,
Even if it's the last thing you do

THE REASON I WRITE . . .

Writing in solace,
   Writing as a soul
Writing to find a place,
Where I finally feel whole
Writing to express my thoughts,
In reality, they're all I've got
Writing to shed the last tear,
Writing to erase the blurry truth,
And make it clear
Writing to feel and believe,
In that untouched and innocent me
Writing to erase thee,
Writing to feel free
As free,
As an injured bird can be.

TRACES

The feel of a pen
Clasped in my hand
The words written on the last page
They still linger,
Thoughts brought to life
Another memory,
Syllables that marked another day,
Another event in my life's history
Emotions invoked by the art
A union of the soul and heart
A rhyme, that ends
With the turn of a page
A hidden grudge
Revealed in the words
That dies without an age
Every feeling, every word
Is lost
In another soul rending
Ink spot,
Another pain, another sorrow
Forgotten and erased
There's just words and ink
Acting as trace.

TRAITS

Truth, Honesty, Faith
  Three traits
I look for,
And people hate,
Justice and truth
To stay pure,
Through the course of my youth
Sincere and brave,
To be able to handle
Situations grave,
To have a heart
To know the right time to start,
To be loyal,
To stay the same for normals
And for royals,
To be strong
And be able to judge,
Right from wrong
To be a hero
Not in a film,
But in real life
To be a better daughter,
A better wife
To spread happiness and joy,
Give a child his favorite toy,
To have a soul,
To make life whole
To walk on this thorny path
And still remain you
To yourself, you must be true.

VEILED

Hiding my incapability,
Under the veil of a smile
Hiding the intensity of my feelings,
Somewhere deep inside,
The core of my heart is dying
I try to lift off,
But these wings, they're not flying
Burdened by my fears,
Soaked in tears
Of abandonment and loneliness,
Walking a path
With utter hopelessness
Why . . .
Why is it so easy,
To break down,
And fade away without a sound,
To vanish and leave no trace
Oh! If only the veil could be lifted off my face.

VICTORIOUS

Burden,
It's what I've been carrying,
The weight of the expectations,
On my shoulders,
The pain, the ache
It never gets older,
It pulls me down,
It breaks my soul,
It rips and tears,
It won't leave me whole,
It fights a war,
With my heart,
It's already conquering,
Though the war's not come to a start,
It triumphs, it seizes,
My heart, it freezes
With it's cold hatred,
But no longer will I silently take it,
I fight with all my strength,
All my heart,
'Till all the remaining shreds of disdain,
Have been torn apart,
I soar in the sky of victory,
'Cuz I've finally broken free,
I float in heaven,
As my soul sets free.

WAGING WARS

Everyday, every minute's
A war
The fight gets harder,
Every hour,
It's a new list,
Of enemies, I need to strike,
It's a new series,
Of surrender and plight,
It's a time of victory,
There's no scope for loss,
It's like this life,
Was a victorious toss,
It's a new feeling,
A bit endearing,
It's a new battle,
More hatred to tackle,
But it's all right,
I'll conquer them all,
With my endless might,
I'll break and crush,
Kill, if I must
To succeed,
It's a taste of triumph,
My soul needs.

WHISPERS

Words and whispers,
Slip away,
The truth struggles
And fades away,
The feeling grows,
And drifts away,
You hold my hand,
And pull away,
You see through me,
And look away,
Is it your ignorance?
Or is it things you can't say?
Is it a dream?
To distant to walk the way,
Is it a loan?
I'm forced to pay,
Is it just a secret?
You'll reveal, if you may,
Or is it just the narration,
In God's unknown play?

WORDS

Words of power,
Words of might
Words that convey
A hopeless plight
Words of strength,
Words that come out wrong
And are not what you meant,
Words of change,
Words of youth
Words that move
And ring of the truth,
Words as hot as fire
Words that burn with desire,
Words yet to bloom
Words that peel away
Shadows of gloom,
Words that fly
Us away to dreams,
Words that relieve
Long withheld screams,
Words that are fighters
Weapons of writers
Trying to be heard,
Trying to be, just more than words
Struggling, spreading
Trying to make you read
The prose, the poetry
A syllable's story.

About the Poet

Mansi Hitesh is a fifteen-year-old girl hoping to touch the world with words inked with a quill. She indulges in coffee, music, and rainy days. The loudest singer in games of Antakshari, the quietest student in Math, she writes about love, laughter, memories, and all the other bizarre emotions that define life as she knows it.